Published in 2015 by Masar Printing and Publishing

ISBN 978-9948-18-151-4

Approved by the National Media Council UAE:

No 23371   08 December 2014

Written by: Marwa Abdelhaleem

بقلم: مروة عبد الحليم

Illustrated by: Ionita Andrei

رسومات: أندريا لوميتا

Translated by: Dr. Tariq Abdelhaleem

ترجمة: د. طارق عبد الحليم

Dedication
إهداء

This book is dedicated to my Baba, the best Baba in the world. You took me
shopping, to the movies and I was your sidekick on Saturday morning errands.
You are a man of your word and that I am truly grateful for.

أهدي هذا الكتاب إلى أبي ، أفضلُ أبٍ في الدنيا، كُنت تأخذني للتسوق ومشاهدةِ الأفلامِ ،
وتصحبني أيام السبت في جولاتكَ ، أنت أبّ بكل معاني الكلمة ، وأنا فخورةٌ بذلك.

Asiya Atcha, thank you for taking time and effort to help
perfect this book in the making. You are a friend like no other.

آسيا آتشا، جزاكي اللهُ، خيراً على أعطاكِ الوقتَ والجهدَ لإخراج هذا الكتاب،
وأنا أعتزُ بصداقتك.

أبي أفضلُ صديقٍ لي

My Baba and I are best friends.

رافَقَتِي دائِمًا مِنَ الصَّباح إلى اْلمَساء

We talk to each other from morning until the day ends.

أَتَعَلَّمُ مِنْ بابا ما هُوَ الصَّحْ و ما هُوَ الْخَطَأ

My Baba teaches me what is wrong and what is right.

أُحَدِّثُهُ عَنْ أَسْراري فَيَحْفَظُها

We tell each other secrets and promise to keep them tight.

نشعرُ بالسعادة عندما نقرأُ القصص

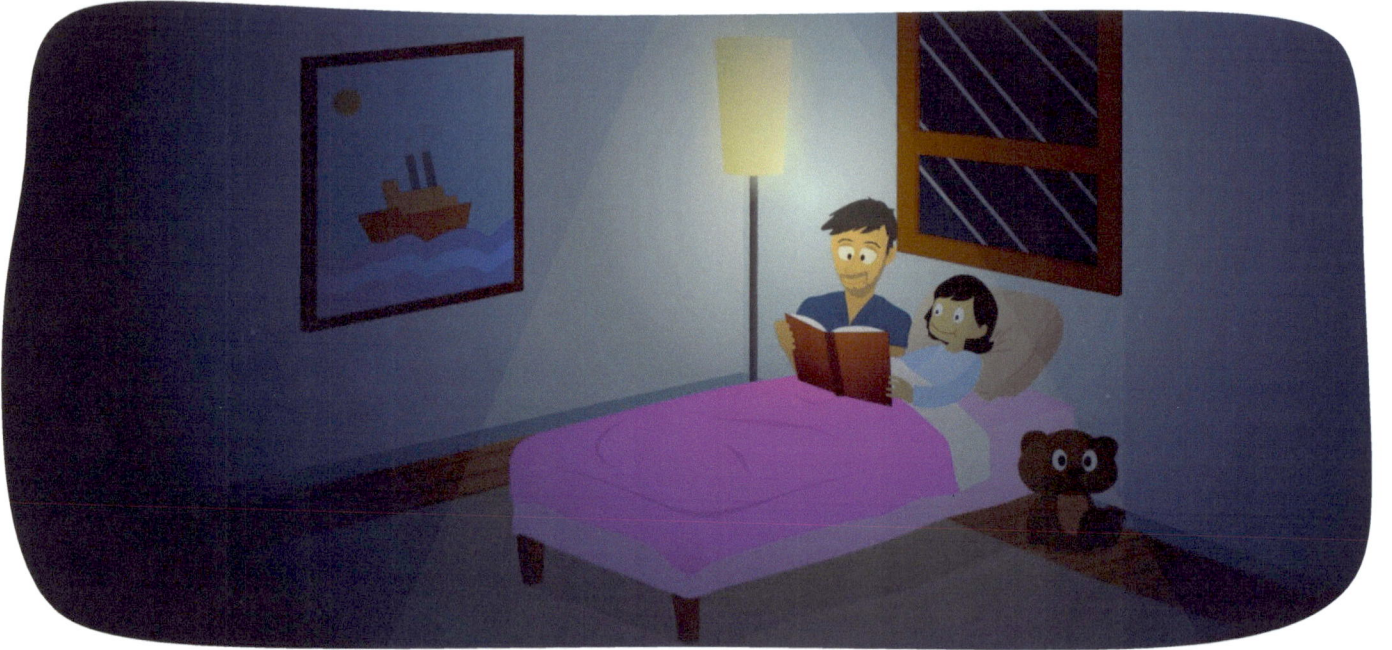

We laugh together, reading a story or

ونطَيِّرُ طائرةً ورقيةً

flying a kite.

نَبْني أَبراجًا عالِيَة بالْمُكَّعباتِ ما أَجْمَلَها !

We build tall towers together; what a delight!

نَتَسابَقُ مَعًا وَ نَقْفِزُ فوقَ الصُّخور

We race together, jumping over rocks

نَخْتَبِئُ بينَ الأشْجار

and running under trees.

نُهَرولُ في الْغَابَةِ وَنَلْعَبُ لُعْبة اَلْفارس واَلْمَلِكةِ

As Knight and Queen we stumble in the forest,

نَضْحَكُ كَثِيرًا فَنَجْلِسُ على رُكْبَتَينا مِنْ شِدِةِ الضَّحِكِ

giggling as we land on our knees.

نَعودُ إلى الْبيتِ لِنَطْبخَ الطَّعام

When we go home, we cook together

نَطْبُخُ ٱلْكَثِيرَ مِنَ ٱلْمَعْكرونَةِ و ٱلْجْبْن

making lots of macaroni and cheese.

نُشَكِّلُ وُجوهًا مُضْحِكَة أمام المرآةِ

Sometimes we make funny faces together

آه ...كان يجبُ أنْ أقولَ لبابا لو سمحت

when I remember to say please!

نصومَ شهرَ رمضان كلهُ

We fast the whole month of Ramadan

ولا نأكلُ حتى غروبِ الشمسِ

and don't eat or drink until sunset, which makes us feel as light as a feather.

When it's time to break our fast,

نَكونُ جائِعين لدرجةِ اَّننا نَظُنُ بِأَنا سَوفَ نَأْكُلُ إلى الابِد

we are so hungry we want to eat forever.

وَبَعْد رَمَضانَ نَفْرحُ وَنحْتَفِلُ بِالْعيد

When Ramadan is over, we celebrate Eid

نلعبُ في الخارج أيا كانَ الجو

and play outside, no matter the weather.

بابا هوَ أفضلُ صديقٍ لي

My Baba is my best friend, now and forever

بابا دائماً معي حتى لو كانَ بعيداً

...even when we are not together.

Marwa Abdelhaleem, author

Marwa Abdelhaleem, a Canadian citizen with an Egyptian heritage, currently resides and works in the United Arab Emirates. She graduated from the University of Phoenix in the United States of America with a Masters Degree in Curriculum and Instruction. Marwa is a licensed Kindergarten teacher who is currently employed as Head of Faculty in a school in the Abu Dhabi Emirate. She has begun working on a second book, which tentatively explores the relationship between a mother and her young son.

المؤلف مروة عبد الحليم :
مواطنة كندية متحدرة من جّذورمصرية ، مقيمة في دولة الإمارات، تخرجت من جامعة فينكس في الولايات المتحدة الأمريكية، وتحمل درجة الماجستير في المناهج التعليمية، وتعمل حاليا رئيسة لقسم في إحدى مدارس ابو ظبي، كما انها تحمل ترخيصا في التدريس الأولي ، وقد بدأت في اعداد كتابها الثاني والذي يتناول العلاقة بين الأم وطفلها.

www.ingramcontent.com/pod-product-compliance
Lightning Source LLC
Chambersburg PA
CBHW042118040426
42449CB00002B/95

9 789948 181514